I0060503

revolutionary
productivity

How to **Maximize** Your
Time, Impact, and **Income**
in Your Small Business

KATIE MAZZOCCO

Copyright © Katie Mazzocco, 2016
All rights reserved.

No part of this publication may be reproduced, stored in a retrieval
system, or transmitted in any form or by any means, electronic,
mechanical, photocopying, recording, scanning, or otherwise, except as
permitted under Section 107 or 108 of the 1976 United States Copyright
Act, without the prior written permission of the publisher. Requests to
publisher for permission should be addressed to Katie Mazzocco, P.O.
Box 12733, Pittsburgh, PA, 15241, United States; or by e-mail at info@
fullspectrumproductivity.com.

Limit of liability/Disclaimer of Warranty: The Publisher makes no
representation or warranties with respect to the accuracy or completeness of
the contents of this work and specifically disclaims all warranties, including
without limitation warranties of fitness for a particular purpose. No warranty
may be created or extended by sales or promotional materials. The advice
and strategies contained herein may not be suitable for every situation. This
work is sold with the understanding that the Publisher is not engaged in
rendering legal, accounting, counseling, or other professional services. If
such assistance is required, the services of a competent professional should
be sought. Neither the Publisher nor the Editor shall be liable for damages
arising herefrom. The fact that an Author's organization or web site is
referred to in this work as a potential source of further information does not
mean that the Publisher endorses the information the organization or web
site may provide, or recommendations it may make.

ISBN-13: 978-0997714302
ISBN-10: 0997714301

Library of Congress Control Number:

Cover Design: Marianna Zotos
Editing & Interior Design: Bryna René Haynes
                    www.TheHeartofWriting.com

Printed in the United States.

Dedication

To my husband, Jess, the love of my life. Thank you for your unwavering support, and for always believing in me 1000 percent, even when I don't believe in myself.

And to my mother, Gloria, who taught me to follow my intuition above all else. I'm grateful that you modeled for me how to immediately love every soul I encounter on the path of life, wrap them in dignity, and never judge.

Resources

Join the growing number of revolutionary entrepreneurs using Katie's seven-step **Revolutionary Productivity Process**, which guarantees that you will save *two hours per day or more* in your small business!

Revolutionary Productivity Academy™
www.RevolutionaryProductivityAcademy.com

Mission-passionate entrepreneurs join the **Revolutionary Productivity Academy** not only to save *two or more hours per day* in their businesses, but also to discover exactly how to make more money, transform the world in a bigger way, and get their lives back.

Using the **Revolutionary Productivity Process,** you can stop burning out and have the life and business you dream of. Through this six-month online academy, you too can revolutionize your productivity in a loving, supportive community of passionate entrepreneurs.

Visit the link above to learn more!

On Social Media

Facebook: www.Facebook.com/FSProductivity

Twitter: www.Twitter.com/FSProductivity

YouTube: www.YouTube.com/FSProductivity

LinkedIn: www.linkedin.com/in/klmazzocco

Katie is active on Facebook, Twitter, YouTube and LinkedIn. She loves to engage in meaningful conversations, inspire and support entrepreneurs in leading the lives they dream of. Visit the links above to connect today.

Book Katie to Speak!

Book Katie as your next keynote speaker and you're certain to revolutionize your productivity while discovering how to maximize your time, impact, and income in your small business.

Katie Mazzocco has been leading, laughing with and inspiring audiences for more than four years, and has helped thousands with her energetic and results-oriented messages. She believes that entrepreneurs are here to transform the world and it's her mission and passion to help small business owners, like you, transform more lives by being more productive.

As the creator of the **Revolutionary Productivity Process** and founder of the **Revolutionary Productivity Academy,** Katie is resolute in her belief that people, especially entrepreneurs, are not meant to be productivity-machines.

Your productivity and "success" should not be measured and scrutinized by cold inputs and outputs, rather your productivity should be defined by what Katie defines as **The Revolutionary Zone.** From this place your business, personal life and mission find balance and sustainability, which prevents you from falling victim to **The Cycle of Burnout**.

Her expertise has been sought out by the award-winning learning platform, Curious.com, where she is their resident small business productivity expert.

For more information, visit
www.FullSpectrumProductivity.com/speaking

Contents

Introduction

The world needs more love.

Period. End of Story.

You might wonder: what does this have to do with small business?

The world needs more entrepreneurs who are clear on why they're here. Entrepreneurs who are willing to transform and rise to their calling—who are willing and eager to disintegrate the barriers between them and the fullest expression of their mission. The world needs warriors who are willing to look resistance in the face, take a true assessment of their limiting habits and beliefs, and revolutionize themselves into the powerhouses they are destined to become.

If this is you, this book is your path.

If this is you, this book is your battle cry.

If this is you, this book is your step-by-step map to the deep, wide, abundant success you so ardently desire.

A Business Is Only As Successful As Its Systems

Imagine that the company you dream of building is actually a city you are designing. You envision beautiful buildings, sparkling sidewalks, people smiling, clear air, and parks filled with children's laughter. But what does your city need to have in order to support these things? What is foundational for its success?

Your city needs *systems*. It needs organization and processes like water lines, electricity, gas lines, roads, parks, and even waste removal. (Isn't that sexy?) While designing a city seems like it should be a lot more fun than thinking about systems, organization, and processes, these things are essential for the function and growth of your budding metropolis. Without systems and processes, trash would pile up, people would go thirsty, and no one would want to live there.

The same is true of your business. In order to create a thriving, lasting company, you must have systems and routine processes that support your productivity, grow your company, and maximize your impact in the world.

Why My Process Is Different

You may be asking, "How is this any different than all of the other productivity strategies and systems out there?" The difference is that, while other strategies focus on output and activity, I focus on maximizing *impact*.

I don't believe that people are meant to be machines.

My goal is not to cram as much activity and output into your days as humanly possible. Rather, I believe life and business should be designed for enjoyment. When small business owners are fulfilled (meaning, they are filled up with joy, ease and love), that fulfillment overflows contagiously to all those in their sphere, and things start to catch fire in a *good* way.

The goal of this book is to equip you to begin to build custom systems, structures, and processes that suit the industry, niche, and business structure of your company. By doing this, you will be able to turn up the volume on your impact in the world in a sustainable way.

When I say "impact," I don't mean that you are a non-profit, in a "helping" profession, or even that you're a philanthropist (although one or all of those things may be true for you). What I mean is that you are equipped with the perfect gifts and talents to change the lives of people who need *exactly* what you do. Whether you're a coach, consultant or service-based small business owner, the world needs you.

The path to transforming the world and increasing your income is the same— it is about leveraging your time, team, and technology. If you are working one-to-one—or if you are the only one in your company—there is a limit to your reach. If you have a team, but the technology or systems you're using are not maximizing your time, energy, and output, the same is true. You don't know what you don't know.

If you continue on the path you're on—working too many hours, not seeing the results you desire, sacrificing leisure time or time with your family, or letting your health fall to the wayside—what do you think will happen? Is that truly sustainable?

My guess is that, if you are reading this book, it's not. You are ready to discover a new way—a better way—of doing things.

I can help you do that.

Let's be honest: if your company isn't sustainable, it probably won't survive. If most entrepreneurs continue down the path they are on now, they will either burn out, run out of money, or give up. According to Forbes and Bloomberg, eight out of ten small businesses fail in the first eighteen months.[1] Of those that make it beyond that point, (according to the Small Business Administration), only fifty percent will survive the next five years.[2]

I've dedicated my own work to helping small business owners like you survive the odds. Through this book, I want to help you take a stand for yourself and your mission. I believe in you. I know that the world needs your unique gifts.

At the end of the day—or the end of our lives—it's about the change we bring to the world. What change are *you* going to bring? How many people's lives are you positioned to impact right now? Are you ready to turn up the volume?

If you implement what I'm about to teach you in this book, you will begin to enjoy growth in your business, and start to see the impact of a business you've designed with intention. If you choose to continue the work in

(1) Source: http://www.forbes.com/sites/ericwagner/2013/09/12/
five-reasons-8-out-of-10-businesses-fail/#74fb73cb5e3c
(2) Source: https://www.sba.gov/sites/default/files/FAQ_March_2014_0.pdf

this book and enroll in my **Revolutionary Productivity Academy™**, I guarantee that you will save *two or more hours per day* while increasing your income, enjoying more ease, and maximizing your impact in the world.

Whatever path you choose—following the steps in this book, or engaging in the full program—you will get out of this work what you put into it. This process is revolutionary, but there is no magic bullet. If you complain, identify as a victim, make excuses, or do things halfway, you will receive weak results or no results. However, if you give it your full effort, commit to the process, and take personal responsibility, you'll enjoy the fruits of your labor in both life and business.

Doesn't that sound dreamy?

I thought so.

I believe you can do this, and I understand where you are. For me, balancing my roles as a business owner, wife, mom of twins, and soul-engaged individual can feel like a formidable task. Over the past few years I've also been on a complex healing journey in my health. Yes, it's complicated sometimes. No, it's not impossible. You just need to remain aware, and remember that you are not alone.

I've created a proven process that works, and I'm going to share it with you—but before I do, I want to check in about where you are right now. Then, I want to show you the positive places you'll be going, and the possibilities for the revolutionized you.

Let's begin.

Chapter 1
Where You Are

The best word to describe where you are right now is *stuck*.

You likely feel as though you are on a hamster wheel of overwhelm. You want to expand, but don't know how. Growth feels like the ultimate catch-22: you aren't growing because you don't feel like you have time, and you're afraid that if you do grow, you'll have even less time! Frustrating!

The list of tasks that fill your time is endless: marketing, following up, networking, e-mail, serving clients, social media, learning, filing, connecting, serving, writing, learning, troubleshooting technology, answering phone calls, business development, planning ... and so much more.

According to Inc.com, 33 percent of small business owners work more than fifty hours per week, while 25 percent work more than sixty hours per week! A mind boggling 70 percent say that they work at least one weekend a month.[1]

Many small business owners I know are stuck in this cycle—what I call **The Cycle of Burnout**.

The Cycle of Burnout™ Consists of Four Phases:

1. Being solely responsible or overly responsible in your business
2. Overworking
3. Getting sick or exhausted, and
4. Investing an insufficient amount of time on healing and recuperating

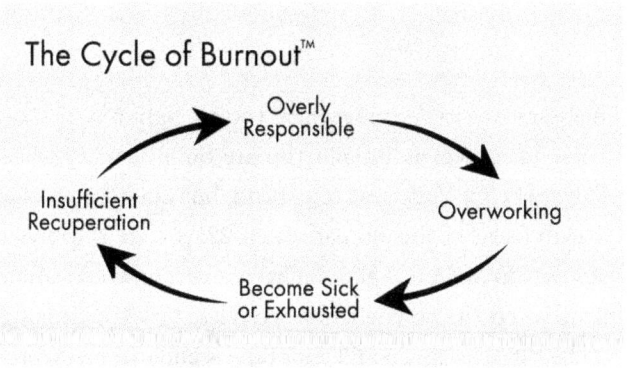

If you've been repeating this cycle for weeks, months or years, it's possible that you've begun to resent your business. It's possible you've even begun to dread your day-to-day existence because you know how hard it is to make it through each day.

It doesn't have to be so hard.

In addition to cycles of burnout, many entrepreneurs I interact with are stuck in deep patterns of unproductivity. When you're always overwhelmed, it's easy to believe that there's nothing you can do to change course. You start to blame yourself, and feel desperately alone in your struggle.

You've likely tried to be more productive and shift the

trajectory of your company, but ended up frustrated by your efforts—as though you were struggling to put out a raging fire with a bucket of water and a teaspoon.

The good news is, it *isn't your fault*. When you first start a company, it is nearly impossible to know how to organize and structure your small business for optimal, sustainable productivity at each stage of growth, and during the treacherous transition times between those growth stages. They don't teach these skills in school—not even in business school. You can't expect yourself to magically know what you need to know.

But even if you understand that it's not your fault, you probably feel guilty, because you want to impact more lives, and make more profit to support your family. You may be accumulating debt in your attempts to "get it right," or simply struggling with the dissatisfaction of doing tedious tasks all day that feel totally unconnected to your core passion.

Here's the truth: by trying to be and do everything in your business, you are working against your natural wiring and not honoring your gifts. Would you want your car mechanic to bake your bread, or your accountant to take over your graphic design work? Probably not.

The Self-Made Millionaire Myth

It is easy to buy into the poisonous myth that you can be a self-made millionaire, but have news for you. "Self-made" is a fallacy, and a recipe for failure. I know many millionaires, and not a single one of them is self-made.

They all strategically built systems, and hired teams of people to support their mission and grow their company.

For a long time, I thought that delegating was a weakness. I thought it was a waste of money. I thought that I wasn't a good entrepreneur if I needed help. However, after studying with top entrepreneurs, I learned the deep error of my convictions and shifted my beliefs around this crucial part of small business ownership. Delegation is now one of my favorite superpowers as an entrepreneur.

Maybe you are afraid to delegate because you don't know how what to delegate first, or how to find someone who's a good fit for your company and "onboard" them in a way that invites them to produce the exceptional results you expect. Or, maybe you think that it will take more time and energy to manage a team than to just do it yourself. There are a lot of scary unknowns—and honestly, there aren't many people teaching you how to address them.

Delegation is just one of the many new skills you'll learn in this book. Another is organization.

If you're like most entrepreneurs, your office is disorganized, your to-do list is overflowing (and in twenty different locations), your calendar isn't organized efficiently, and you're beyond overcommitted. Due to your lack of time and energy, you are likely subconsciously—or even overtly—repelling opportunities. Maybe you resist following up with leads. Maybe you brush off the opportunity for a joint venture partnership. Maybe you let deadlines for media exposure fly by. These missed opportunities slowly chip away at your confidence and undermine the impact of your mission in the world, not to mention your income.

I get it, though. Sometimes these constant opportunities feel like an assault on your battle-weary soul. You're just trying to survive. Scarcity thinking is starting to infiltrate your mind. (Maybe it feels like hopelessness? Maybe like doubt? It can take so many forms.)

All of the "pain points" outlined above create the picture of where you are now: in overwhelming frustration, disorganization, and fear.

The great news is that it doesn't have to be this way. Change is possible.

You are ready to embrace your inner phoenix—to joyously and easily burn away that which doesn't serve you, and embrace the new, vibrant embodiment of your company and your mission in the world.

In other words, you're ready to *revolutionize*!

Let's talk about what's possible.

Chapter 2
The Revolutionized You

As you implement my seven-step process for Revolutionary Productivity, you'll begin to experience increased income, impact, and available time.

If you wholeheartedly and earnestly implement the basic steps of the **Revolutionary Productivity Process™** outlined in this book, you will start saving time in your business right away.

What Could This Look Like In Your Business?

I'm going to paint a picture for you.

Visualization is a powerful tool that can pull you into your new reality, so let's take a moment to imagine your new "normal."

Your day-to-day business operations have a sense of effortlessness, and you're amazed at what you can accomplish in a week. What used to require your deep concentration and energy is now routinely taken care of by your team and technology.

Your systems and structures for key actions in your company—such as marketing, sales, and client nurturing—are constantly running on autopilot.

Your office and computer feel organized. Communication with your team is systematic and easy. Your inbox is clear and organized. Your calendar and to-do list are in harmony with your goals, and are focused on an equal balance of money-making activities, strategic visioning, and rest.

You are confident and relaxed in your delegating, knowing that you've trained your team appropriately, and that there are systems in place to support them.

When the time comes to expand your team, you are confident that you know how to use key diagnostic tools to identify who is a good fit for your company.

Everyone on your team—including you—only does what they enjoy and are fabulous at.

Your mind feels light and open. With your to-do list perfectly tracked outside of your head, you have space for innovation and decisiveness in your decision making.

You feel nurtured and supported. You know that you have a solid organization behind you that believes in your mission and is committed to sharing it in the world.

You feel a sense of security. Your company is thriving. You are enjoying your increased income and impact in the world.

Most of all, you feel like you're running your company—not like it's running you.

From this new place of ease, you look back on how you used to run your company and recognize that everything that wasn't a part of your distinct gifts was a dirty rock in your backpack, weighing you down as you tried to scale the thrilling mountain of world transformation.

Your company is now a beautiful representation of what you're distinctly good at.

Your world is filled with infinite possibility.

Chapter 3

The Revolutionary Productivity Process™

In my more than fourteen years of small business experience, I've seen many smart and innovative people struggle to move forward.

It can be ugly, really ugly. Small businesses, if not well-managed, can crumble people's self-esteem, finances, relationships, families, and marriages, and even cause them to abandon their dreams.

On the other hand, I've also seen how beautiful and easeful building a business can be. It requires hard work, determination and commitment—but that work is *inspired*, and generates rich rewards like confidence, financial abundance, vibrant relationships, freedom, and the deep peace of being aligned with your purpose.

You must remember that, as you grow your business, *you won't know what you don't know*. What used to work might suddenly stop working, or even hold you back. If you want to say goodbye to overwhelm and feeling stuck, you need to continually evaluate and release these old patterns.

So let today be the day you start fresh, and rebirth your business in a world-transforming and soul-edifying way.

The Revolutionary Productivity Process™

Now, I'm going to show you the tools and strategies of my **Revolutionary Productivity Process** in the exact order they must be implemented to achieve your dreams

This system is the distillation of my years of small business expertise—a simple yet profound seven-step process that will revolutionize your productivity and thereby revolutionize your business, your life, and the world.

Here are the seven sequential steps in my Revolutionary Productivity Process:

1. Set Yourself Free

2. Eliminate Chaos

3. TnT

4. Document Systems

5. Decide to Delegate

6. Commit & Grow

7. Adapt for Success

In the following chapters, I will share with you what each step involves, show you why it's important, and give you actionable steps you can use to start your personal revolution right now!

While you read, I ask that you honor three simple requests:

First, be open-minded about the concepts I am about to share. No matter how simple (or complex) they may seem at first glance, they are proven and irrefutable keys to transformation.

Second, be light-hearted as you read. It may sound crazy, but this process is going to be fun! My clients and I laugh constantly. We actively look for the humor in everyday business situations—even the challenging ones.

Third, whatever happens, please don't berate yourself for not already knowing this stuff, and don't stress about how much work there is to be done. As best-selling author and inspirational speaker Danielle LaPorte says, "Absolutely everything is progress."

The fact that you're even reading this is progress. Approach this process with curiosity and humor, and watch how it changes your world.

Are you ready to *revolutionize*?

Chapter 4

Set Yourself Free

(REVOLUTIONARY PRODUCTIVITY PROCESS™ STEP ONE)

The core of *Set Yourself Free* is to evaluate what is not working in your business and life, especially with regard to where you spend your time and energy. The goal of this process is to take a discerning look into your priorities and boundaries in life and business.

You may be wondering why I keep asking you to consider your life outside of your business. I mean, this is a *business* book, right? Well, yes, it is—but I believe there is a concrete trifecta in small business that creates the revolutionary life and freedom you crave.

Imagine three interlinked circles. The first contains small business systems and productivity, the second soul satisfaction, and the third living a life of love (which I also sometimes describe as living a life of service). The meeting point of these circles is **The Revolutionary Zone™**.

Each of these circles supports the other two. In order to sustain a revolutionary life and business, all three must be in perfect harmony. Without one of them, the ecosystem crumbles.

I created a process called **The Freedom Matrix™**, in which you identify what isn't working, release what isn't serving you, and rewrite your priorities and boundaries

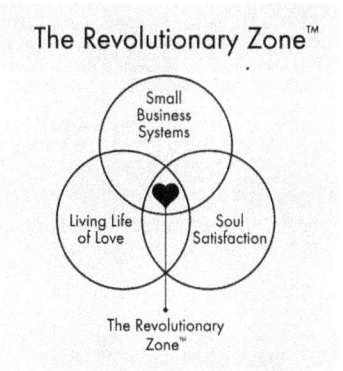

The Revolutionary Zone™

Small Business Systems

Living Life of Love

Soul Satisfaction

The Revolutionary Zone™

to align with the truth of your true desires and goals. This matrix enables you to align with your unique **Revolutionary Zone.**

This process is essential to the success of the **Revolutionary Productivity Process.**

Not only does it challenge the status quo, but it creates a whole new pool of time and energy for you to implement the next six steps of the process.

The Freedom Matrix™

It's important that you dig deep when you're creating new priorities and boundaries. Nothing is off limits. You must challenge everything you consider to be a "have to," a "must," a "commitment," or a "responsibility."

The majority of entrepreneurs I know chose their career paths for the freedom—whether that be time, money, adventure, service to others, or autonomy—but, ironically, many of them find themselves trapped in the expectations and limitations of their friends, families, colleagues, and their own subconscious minds.

Over the years I've found that there are particular words and phrases which serve as masks for other people's priorities—priorities that have been imposed upon you, and that you've accepted as your own. These same words and phrases can also reveal your own limiting beliefs—the things you want to change but are afraid to (or don't feel you have permission to).

Thoughts To Challenge:

- I do _____ because that's the way my family/ friends/community/organization does it.

- I do _____ because that's the kind of person/ family I am.

- I do _____ because that's what a good parent/ spouse/sibling/friend/colleague does.

- I do _____ because it makes my spouse/parents/ kids/colleagues/friends happy.

- I do _____ because it's what _____ wants.

- I do _____ because I don't want _____ to be upset with me.

- I do _____ because it's what I've always done.

- I do _____ because it used to work really well.

Never do something just because it works for someone else. Do it because it works for *you*. I'm not saying that all of these statements are things you need to change. I'm simply sharing them as prime examples of beliefs that mask commitments and tolerations that trap people—especially entrepreneurs—in cycles of unproductivity and overwhelm. This isn't about "right" and "wrong"; it's about awareness.

Challenge everything. Then *choose* what you want.

Time Drains and Time Banks

One way to better understand **The Freedom Matrix Process** is to consider the process of eliminating "time drains" and creating "time banks."

A time drain is something that siphons your time. You might currently be resigned to (or completely unaware of) many of your time drains—but since we all have a finite amount of time in each day, it's important to identify these drains and eliminate them.

A time bank is a place where you discover newly available time that you can then invest in a new way. It's like creating a strategic spending plan and then suddenly having "extra" money that you can spend or invest in other places.

Here's an example of how you can turn a time drain into a time bank. Imagine that you are "expected" to hold your position on a networking group board of directors, even though it no longer inspires or fulfills you. You continue to do it because that's what everyone expects, or you don't want to rock the boat. In **The Freedom Matrix** process, you identify this position as a time drain. You may choose to release the obligation altogether or scale back slowly—but the new space you've created as a result will become a time bank with new investment opportunities.

Now let's break down **The Freedom Matrix Process** that will help you turn time drains into time banks:

The Freedom Matrix Process™

1. **Examine:** Identify what isn't working or doesn't bring you joy.

2. **Release:** Release what isn't serving you.

3. **Redefine:** Rewrite your priorities and boundaries to align with your true desires and goals.

4. **Educate & Align:** Educate those in your life and slowly align with your new priorities and boundaries.

5. **Enjoy:** Begin to enjoy the freedom of living life and running your business on your own terms.

Begin **The Freedom Matrix Process** with Step One. This is a progressive process, so if you skip around through the steps it won't be effective.

To **Examine**, do a deep soul search. Set some time aside for yourself, ideally several hours. Do something that centers, grounds, and inspires you. It is important that you come from a mind-space of abundance and that you are connected with the passion that inspired you to start your company in the first place.

Then, write out everything you are tolerating in your company, personal life, and family—and I mean *everything,* even if you think it seems petty or small. Remember, even microscopic cracks can cause big leaks in the enormous swimming pool of your life and business, so be brutally, lovingly honest during this process.

Some of my clients' lists have been hundreds of items long; others have been merely dozens. The length of your list is irrelevant—but the honesty, intention, and trust that go into it are key.

Once you've completed this examination, you'll be ready to continue to Steps 2 - 5 of **The Freedom Matrix Process**.

It's important to note that, if you skip over **The Freedom Matrix Process**, resist doing it fully, or gloss over those micro-cracks and tiny time drains, you will set yourself up for failure in the subsequent steps of **The Revolutionary Productivity Process**. Why? Because instead of creating new energy and time banks to invest in your business, you'll begin your experience by adding yet another item to your already overflowing to-do list.

Sound like fun? No. Sound like a recipe for success? No. It sounds like **The Cycle of Burnout.** So choose to get off the crazy train here and now, by taking the time to look at what's *really* happening in your life and business.

The beautiful thing about **The Freedom Matrix Process** is that it enables you to get to the heart of what is and isn't working, release everything that doesn't serve, and pick up everything you've always wanted. I like to think of it as a divine exchange between two hands—letting go and receiving at the same time for the highest good of all.

No matter what industry you are in, this process can and will apply to you.

It is safe.

It is your path to freedom.

You can do it. I give you permission.

Chapter 5
Eliminate Chaos

(REVOLUTIONARY PRODUCTIVITY PROCESS™ STEP TWO)

According to the Merriam-Webster Dictionary, the definition of chaos is "complete confusion and disorder."

There are many different kinds of chaos. Some of the primary types involving your **Revolutionary Zone** are:

- Cognitive (in your head)

- External (people around you)

- Physical (physical surroundings)

- Emotional (feelings)

- Intention (desires and goals)

- Energetic (the energy you put out into the world)

In this step of **The Revolutionary Productivity Process,** you will eliminate all of the different types of chaos in your life by looking at them side-by-side and strategically aligning them.

One of the biggest mistakes I see entrepreneurs make is planning, strategizing, and setting intentions and goals in a vacuum. What I mean by this is that small business owners normally set income goals, then separately set their work schedule, and then separately map out their personal schedule. Additionally, if they have a team, they plan their team members' schedules separately. They even make hiring decisions without considering any of these other areas. Everything is decided in a vacuum.

Many people consider separate goal-setting to be focused and logical, but it's not. It is a deep problem, especially when growing a successful small business.

If you set income goals that require you to work sixty hours a week and don't consider your work schedule or personal life, you are setting yourself up for failure. Based on your decisions about your income goals, you need to work twenty more hours more per week than you want to, and sacrifice your personal schedule because it doesn't align with your income goals. When you start losing your mind trying to keep up with the workload, you hire a team member to try to balance the chaos—but after you hire this person (which you did without considering your income goals or personal schedule), you recognize it as a mistake, because your business model isn't sustainable and you need to pivot. It's a lose-lose-lose-lose-lose situation.

To create sustainability in your business, you need to remember that every time you change something in one area it will impact *all other areas* of your life and business, especially in relation to your two most precious resources, time and energy.

The Chaos Conquering Exercise™:

I created the **Chaos Conquering Exercise** to solve the problem of chaos and discord in the multiple areas of your life and business, and equip you to make empowered and strategic course corrections.

1. **Identify Your Sectors:** Make a list of all the different sectors in your life where you plan or have obligations. The most common sectors are:
   - Your income goals
   - Your work schedule
   - Your work goals
   - Upcoming launches
   - Your personal life schedule
   - Your personal goals
   - Your travel schedule for work and pleasure
   - Your health and fitness
   - Each team member's schedule and goals
   - Your hiring and growth strategic plan

2. **Get Clarity:** Using blank calendar sheets for a standard week (or even a standard month), block your daily, weekly, and monthly activities for each sector.

3. **Align:** After completing the calendar sheets, look at them as a collective. See what conflicts arise when your individual sectors meet.

4. **Shift:** After identifying points of conflict, brainstorm alternatives and create solutions so that all of the sectors of your life are in alignment.

5. **Enjoy:** Once you have Aligned and Shifted your commitments, expectations and way of functioning, a path of freedom and ease is yours to enjoy.

If you're still having trouble understanding what I mean about aligning schedules and commitments, imagine old-school transparencies—you know, the kind that were used with projector screens. The goal of the **Chaos Conquering Exercise** is that, if you were to print your schedules and goals onto transparencies and lay them on top of each other, you would project an organized image where all of the components work together. True alignment.

The beautiful part of this process is that it doesn't require you to massively overhaul your company and life. Instead, you will identify what you need to tweak or pivot. It also gives you new perspective on how to be strategic in every part of your life.

This process is foundational in liberating you from the old paradigm of needing to be a money-making machine, focused on a singular goal as your life, body, and business go down in flames around you. It doesn't have to be that way. You aren't meant to be a machine.

Intuition

Once you've created an aligned vision and plan, the second part of Step Two: Eliminating Chaos is to develop and own your intuition.

Intuition is the ultimate superpower in business. If you aren't already listening to your intuition and regularly using your business acumen, you are hindering your ability to succeed and enjoy your life and your business.

Take, for example, the famous entrepreneur, Mark Cuban, on the award-winning television show *Shark Tank*. He and the other "sharks" on the show constantly use their exceptional business intuition. They refer to "good feelings" or "bad feelings." They say things like, "I had to follow my gut," or "Something didn't feel right." When they use phrases like this, they are referring to their intuition. They are not solely relying on logic, strategy, and planning to make high-stakes business decisions, but are instead taking into account an instinctive hunch.

Your intuition should be well developed, and respected as a vital force in your decision-making. Once you have intuition on board as a daily tool in your business, you'll be able to use it to give a power boost to your **Chaos Elimination Exercise**. This will help you align more deeply with your highest good, and the highest good of all. (To discover my favorite strategy for developing your intuition watch this video on my blog: http://bit.ly/intuitiontool)

Without the energetic alignment of these two components, Chaos Elimination and Intuition, creating a revolutionary company and life is impossible. Without alignment, you're going to sabotage yourself. You won't put your whole heart into what you're creating, because subconsciously you'll know you're fighting a losing battle.

Step One of the **Revolutionary Productivity Process**, *Set Yourself Free*, showed you how to create space to sculpt and hone your revolutionary path. In Step Two, *Chaos Elimination*, you aligned all of the various sectors of your life and business. Now, it's time to "blow it up" into massive success with Step Three, *TnT*.

Chapter 6

TnT™

Yes, you read that right: *TnT*™ is Step Three. It's time to blow things up in an amazing way. This step will multiply all of the goodness you created in Steps One and Two, and exponentially increase the impact of Steps Four through Seven as well.

TnT stands for "Time Management 'n' Task Management." This step is all about taking an inspired and surgical look at how your calendar and your to-do list intersect.

You're likely similar to the overwhelming majority of entrepreneurs in that your calendar and to-do lists are not only overflowing, but tragically unconnected. The twenty things you want to accomplish today are not reflected on your calendar, and your calendar is full of too many other commitments.

In order to accomplish everything on your plate, you'd have to clone yourself, sleep less, or accept failure because more hours just can't be added to your day. What do you do in this situation? Do you cancel your commitments to your family? Do you deprive yourself of sleep? Do you push back deadlines? Do you panic? Do you berate yourself for never being enough? No matter how you slice this pie, you only get disappointment and frustration.

If you aren't managing your tasks well, you will miss opportunities. When your mind is constantly trying to track and juggle what needs to be done, time and energy are wasted. It may feel as if you are putting all of your time, energy and money into a sieve and watching it flow away from you. This process erodes your confidence and energy reserves, eventually leading to **The Cycle of Burnout**.

Managing Your Time

The first focus of *TnT* is managing your time for maximum impact and enjoyment in both your business and life. Time is a finite resource. Beyond having a set number of hours in each day, we all have a certain amount of time in our lives, which is unknown to us. Luckily, you have the power to invest your time strategically and powerfully.

My all-time favorite illustration of the time available to each of us in our lives is the brilliant video by Ze Frank. In the video, "The Time You Have (in Jelly Beans)," Ze uses 28,835 jellybeans to visually portray how many days the average American has in their lives. He then goes on to break down the amount of time we spend doing various activities in our lives. So moving. So inspiring. I highly suggest every entrepreneur watch it. (Here's the link: http://bit.ly/jellybeantime)

TnT is all about how you manage and track your time. If you plan to grow your company to change the world, you will need to delegate. And if you want to delegate, you need to be able to communicate with your team easily and succinctly, so that they can be productive and effective.

This requires technology.

Do you use paper calendars, or an electronic or hybrid calendar? Many people are afraid of moving their calendar to an electronic format, but I know of very, very few instances where it is a good decision for a business owner to keep their calendar in paper format.

My clients continuously tell me that, once they took the plunge into electronic time and task management tools, it revolutionized their life and business. They are raving fans! I love taking this journey with them and making the transition as pain-free as possible.

Technology must be used appropriately for maximum efficiency. Do you keep e-mails in your inbox after receiving them? Why? I'd be willing to bet that it's because you still need to take action on them. This means you're using your inbox as a to-do list, which it is not designed to do! This is one of the biggest mistakes entrepreneurs make.

Having a dedicated task management ecosystem is the number one solution for effortlessly delegating to your team (and even yourself).

Your management ecosystem should consist of …

- Tasks
- Task assignments
- Due dates
- Comments
- All links and files that pertain to the tasks

… all contained in one place.

Imagine a world where you can effortlessly communicate to your team without mind-numbing e-mail chains, excessively long meetings, or constant check-ins (aka, micromanagement). Imagine a world where your to-do lists aren't written in a hundred different notebooks, or on a million pieces of paper floating all over your home and office. Envision a task management (to-do list) application that holds all of your projects, a breakdown of project-associated tasks, and checklists for all the systems in your company.

It's possible. This can be your reality. All you need to do is step outside your comfort zone and take a decisive look at your calendar and task management.

Choose the Correct Tools

TnT is not just about putting a task management app on your phone and online. It's about choosing the correct tool for your business, and learning how to use it strategically. Your method should support you, not create more work for you.

Don't you hate it when you try something new, invest a lot of time and energy into learning it, and then find out it doesn't work for what you need? That's the worst. But without knowing the intricacies of each task management application, how can you know which to choose?

I want to help save you time and frustration in this process, so I've done the vetting for you! Instead of browsing all the options, your first action step is to create accounts on the following three time and task management platforms.

Time and task management platforms I recommend:
(Costs range from free to $5 per person.)

- **Task Management:** Asana (www.Asana.com)
- **Time Management:** Google Apps Calendar (http://bit.ly/GoogleAppsCal)
- **Team Communication:** Slack (www.Slack.com)

You might be hitting the panic point right now, fearing that the technology gremlins will battle you to the death. It's okay. Just take it slow. Baby, steps if you need. Get help if you need it. This is a safe place. I've got you.

Migrating all of your to-do lists, team projects, and team conversations to a task management platform will be revolutionary for you. It may not seem like it now, but the liberation and ease you feel will be exhilarating. Structuring your business in this way will revolutionize the way your company does business, thereby creating the potential for you to change more lives than ever before.

Now that you see how deliciously "explosive" strategic time and task management *(TnT)* can be for your business, it's time to take things to the next level.

Next up, Step Four: *Documenting Systems*!

Chapter 7

Documenting Systems

(REVOLUTIONARY PRODUCTIVITY PROCESS™ STEP FOUR)

Ooh! *Documenting Systems*. Sounds sexy, doesn't it?

(Not really, I know.)

The words *documenting* and *systems* may both sound miserable, but once you start creating systems, it will become a healthy addiction. You just won't want to stop.

Creating and documenting systems is one of those time math equations where only one, three, or ten hours of work can yield, tens, hundreds or thousands of saved hours over the future days, weeks, months, and years.

Who doesn't love a time/money equation like that?

There are three goals in Step Four of the Revolutionary Productivity Process:

1. Prevent your mind from having to retain, remember and recall information for activities you do routinely or infrequently in your business.

2. Create a comprehensive tool which allows you to easily delegate to new team members and stop micromanaging current team members.

3. Prevent company knowledge from "walking out the door" when team members move on from your company.

If you are like many entrepreneurs, there are numerous things in your company that you think you could never delegate; maybe you even feel that way about everything.

However, if you can't easily transfer knowledge or train a new person to join your team, you can impair the growth of your company. Many small business owners intelligently hire team members with more expertise than their own in various specialties. This is actually very healthy—but what happens if that team member leaves?

Team member knowledge is part of the foundation your company. When they leave without you having documented their systems, they unintentionally take a part of the foundation of your company with them.

Systems Release Pressure

Imagine your brain as a glass cylinder with a finite amount of space. In the center, there are straws creating a "floor" that suspends a bunch of colored marbles. The marbles represent the things you have to remember and retain every day as a small business owner. (I'll bet that cylinder is just about overflowing.) But what happens when the straws break, and the marbles go flying everywhere?

Systems release the pressure of all of those marbles. As you document your business's systems, you are able to pluck marbles out of the cylinder one by one, eventually leaving a spacious cylinder that is the perfect environment for innovation and strategic leadership.

At this point you may be thinking that creating systems sounds intimidating, and you have no idea where to begin.

The first thing you need to know is that this is not a race. You are not going to systematize your company overnight, so you're off the hook for making this your "one-month goal."

Secondly, you're going to be strategic, and create a system for creating your systems!

Create a list of the activities and process that you do most often, waste the most time on, lose the most money on doing yourself, or struggle with the most. This is your starting point. By documenting challenging systems first, you will get the biggest return on investment of your time, energy and money.

How To Document Systems

"But how, exactly, do I document a system?" you ask.

That's an excellent question!

A "system" is a written documentation of exactly how, what, why, where, and when you do an activity in your business. Most often there is a short written explanation of the system (a paragraph or two) answering what, why, where, and when the activity is done. Then, the bulk of the system is presented as a step-by-step numbered checklist of exactly what actions to take, in the exact order they should be taken, as well as where and how to take them.

Most systems will be sequential. Systems pertaining to creative tasks or decision-making are the exception. In these cases, system documentation can be more informative, with suggestions and insights to guide the process.

Remember, your goal is to write your system so that *anyone* who reads it can do that activity effectively. It is also good to outline "success criteria" for most systems. (In other words, if you do x, y, and z, this process was successful.) For example, if you send out the newsletter by 10:00 a.m. on Tuesday, according to the listed formatting, you will have met the success criteria for the system.

Begin with your high-stress, high-loss systems. Then create a list of everything that you and your team do in a given day or week. Once you have this list, you can craft a strategy for documenting all of the systems.

To get your creative juices flowing, I've shared my list of The Top 33 Systems Every Entrepreneur Must Have to Be Successful on the next page.

The Top 33 Systems Every Entrepreneur Must Have to Be Successful

1. Lead Nurture System
2. Client Intake System
3. Client Service Delivery System
4. Client Nurture System
5. Customer Relationship Management (CRM) System
6. Referral System
7. Testimonial System
8. Customer Service System
9. Networking System
10. Networking Follow-Up System
11. Marketing Calendar System
12. Social Media System
13. E-mail Newsletter System
14. Blog Post System
15. Video Creation System
16. Joint Venture System
17. Press and Media System
18. Project Management System
19. Team Management System
20. Hiring System
21. Firing System
22. E-mail Management System
23. Scheduling System
24. Digital Filing System
25. Filing System
26. Out of Office System
27. Technology Updates System
28. Business Development System
29. Strategic Planning System
30. Bookkeeping System
31. Payroll System
32. Tax System
33. Archive System

The beautiful thing is that, once you document your first system (and if you back it up well), you'll it them forever. Yes, you may need to update the system after a time—but in the meantime, bask in the glory of having documented a system!

One note on formatting: the best place to house an original version of a system is in a Microsoft Word® document. This is due to the universality of the program. Word also enables you to insert images and hyperlinks to websites, video tutorials and cloud files as necessary. Back up your system file in at least three places.

When It Comes To Team Members ...

No matter what type of team member you are thinking about hiring, it is absolutely essential that you document the systems you want that person to perform in your company *before* you hire them.

Many entrepreneurs hope that the team members they hire will magically organize and document their company for them. However, unless that is a distinct talent of the people you are hiring, you cannot expect them to do this for you. It is a unique skill set.

That being said, if you hire someone with more expertise than you in a certain area, you can ask them to build upon the system you already have in place.

In my fourteen years of small business experience, I have worked with many entrepreneurs who are constantly frustrated with their team, some to the point where they are continuously hiring and firing people in an endless cycle. Their team is constantly "new"—and therefore unprepared to meet the expectations placed upon them.

The truth is, the problem isn't the team members. It's that the business owners don't have systems in place to appropriately train and equip team members to excel in their positions. I call this **The Cycle of Scapegoating™**. As an outsider, it's very sad to witness. As a small business owner, it's infuriating, and can lead people to settle for smaller versions of their dream and mission because "no one can help them."

If you've been in this cycle before, it's okay; there is no blame or judgment. Now is the perfect time to break it. I know you can do it. You have a world to change and a mission to grow. Systems are your solution.

At this point, you may still be stressed by idea of documenting systems. Some people literally break out in hives at the thought of it.

I'm here for you if you need help. I have more best practices, tools, and strategies for system documentation than I could ever hope to contain in this book. My "library" currently has more than 250 systems in it, and it grows every week.

Once you have your foundational systems in place, the next logical step is to delegate your systemized tasks and get them off your hands. Luckily, that's exactly what we're going to cover in Step Five!

Chapter 8
Decide to Delegate

When most people think about delegating, they assume that they have to hire a team member. However, that isn't always the case.

There are two distinct ways to delegate in your company. These are to *Technology* and *Team*.

Remember the myth of the self-made millionaire we talked about in Chapter 1? It's still a myth. Whether you are looking at a successful person who makes multiple six figures, seven figures, or beyond, I would bet money that they have systems in their businesses, and delegate regularly to their team and technology. There is no way they could possibly handle all of their marketing, e-mail, website design and maintenance, social media, and client communication on their own.

Without systematizing and deciding to delegate, you will hit a ceiling of finite growth. You won't be able to make any more money. You won't be able to grow your mission. There are temporary ways to cheat fate, but ultimately, it's just physics. There is only so much of you. There are only twenty-four hours in a day, and only so many hours of sleep that you can steal from yourself. There's just no way around multiplying yourself through your technology and your team.

It's possible that you're at a place in your company where you don't have the financial resources to bring on team members. I am not advising you to "jump the gun" and make a choice that would put you or your company in financial jeopardy. Regardless, don't skip this section. Delegating is about making strategic decisions that are in the best interest of your company. I have some ninja strategies to share with you.

Technology

In most situations, I recommend that entrepreneurs delegate to technology before delegating to team members. There are thousands of different technologies and applications on the market, ranging from free to a moderate investment. Depending on your biggest time drains and specific industry, you will likely find several that can immediately start saving you time.

When delegating to either technology or team, the golden rule is measuring the return on investment.

Let's say you are a career coach, and playing e-mail-tag with clients and potential clients eats up anywhere from thirty to ninety minutes of your day. (Crazy town! I get it.) You would love to have an amazing assistant who handles all of your scheduling—but if you're not in the financial position to hire someone, why not delegate your scheduling to an automated online scheduler instead? That way, "scheduling" leads and clients consists of sending them a link to schedule themselves.

BAM! Thirty to ninety minutes of your day, saved!

Here is my five-step process to determine what to delegate first in your company:

1. **Create a List:** Write down the top 10 to 20 time wasters in your company (such as scheduling).

2. **Research:** Type the keyword for what you want to delegate plus the word "application" into your browser's search engine. (To continue our example, this would look like "scheduling application.") Small business owners love to share resources, especially on social media, so ask your colleagues for recommendations, too.

3. **Compare:** Once you have several options, weigh the return on investment for each application based on setup time, learning curve, and features available. If it's something you envision as a long-term solution, I recommend choosing the option that can grow with you, even if it's a bit of a stretch at first.

4. **Commit:** Now that you've strategically compared the options, it's time to commit to one and set it up. Remember, while the time and energy it takes to set it up may be frustrating, this is a solution that is going to create time banks for you in your business. It will be worth it, and it will pay for itself sooner than you think.

5. **Benefit:** Enjoy the newfound time banks in your business. Invest them strategically.

I often help entrepreneurs determine what they need to delegate to technology. Then, I show them how to use delegating to technology as a stepping stone to delegating to a team.

Team

You can ride the momentum of your return on investment from delegating to technology, and start delegating to real people.

Many entrepreneurs choose the easiest thing to delegate first. Don't make this mistake. Instead, choose what's going to make the biggest impact. The momentum generated can then be used to build time, energy, and money for your business.

Here is the foundational sequence you should follow when recruiting, interviewing, and hiring a new team member:

1. Decide what activity or activities to delegate first in your company.

2. Determine what position would be appropriate for the activity or activities you wish to be performed.

3. Write a job description for the position.

4. Write interview questions based on the job description skills, culture and strengths you are looking for.

5. Map out your interview and hiring process, including the hiring timetable, milestones of the interview process you want potential team members to go through, e-mail responses and instructions for each milestone in the interview process, and the onboarding and training process.

6. Write an advertisement for the position.

7. Post the advertisement online.

8. Send applicants acknowledgment, scheduling, and "next steps" e-mails.

9. Conduct round one of interviews.

10. Narrow down the applicants. Notify those who didn't make the cut. Notify the applicants who are moving on to the next stage and give them their next set of instructions.

11. Conduct round two of interviews.

12. Have applicants take assessments to measure their strengths, innate talents, and the ways they are wired for action.

13. Choose who you want to hire, or repeat steps 9 and 10 if you want to narrow your search further.

14. Notify your chosen applicant. In communication, be sure to include the contract, appropriate tax forms, non-disclosure agreement, and details on orientation and training next steps.

15. Notify the applicants who were not accepted.

16. Host an orientation with your new hire.

17. Schedule training for your new hire.

18. Communicate the gradual level of responsibilities your new hire will take on.

Writing a job description can be a stressful undertaking for many small business owners. To get yourself started, Google job descriptions for the position you want to hire for. Gather your favorite examples, then combine them. Remember, the more authentic you are in writing your job description, the more aligned your future hire will be with you and your company's culture.

When interviewing potential hires, it's important to ask questions that will reveal not only their skills and experience, but also their personality, work ethic, and level of commitment and interest. Sometimes, the best hire is someone who lacks in experience, but blows other applicants out of the water in terms of enthusiasm and willingness to learn.

A common mistake small business owners make is to make their position advertisements too "professional." If you are fun and silly, be fun and silly. If you are loving, be loving. If you are particular, be particular. Company culture fit is a crucial factor in the success of your hiring process. The more you are true to yourself and your company's culture, the more likely you will be to attract and hire the perfect person.

Assessments are key tools for mitigating risk when hiring, and are worthwhile investments. By using assessments and correct interview skills, you will be able to make decisive hiring decisions, and ensure that you get people who complement your skills, not duplicate them. Often, somebody whose skill set is a copy of your own will experience the same pitfalls that you do, so if you hire a clone of yourself, you won't necessarily be adding value to your company.

When considering your final applicants, ask them to complete an example task to test their performance.

Beyond just building a team, it's important to have intentional team management and communication styles so that your culture and mission isn't diluted. Before, during, and after training and orientation, make sure that your new hires understand the best ways to ask questions and get support in their new position.

The goal of this step in the **Revolutionary Productivity Process** is to help you hire team members with as much ease and success as possible. You may have noticed that the above 18-step process is the skeleton of a system. It would be easy to transform it into a simple, repeatable system specific to your business, which you can then document as discussed in Step Four.

Once you master this part of the systematizing and delegating process in your company, you could hire ten people for ten different positions without stressing one ounce, just by following the process. It's beautiful.

I'm not saying you should go out and hire ten team members tomorrow. I *am* saying is that "deciding to delegate" is really the tipping point between being a startup company and a company that's beginning to systematically increase its impact and income in the world.

Millionaires aren't *special*. They went through the same growth phases as you are going through right now. This is your opportunity to follow their lead.

You're here to change the world. I believe in you.

Up next: growing your company through *commitment*.

Chapter 9

Commit & Grow

(REVOLUTIONARY PRODUCTIVITY PROCESS™ STEP SIX)

Imagine you are on an expedition climbing Mount Everest. You've faced every challenge you can imagine—but then, when you are just a hundred yards from the summit, you decide to turn back because you're tired.

Would that happen? No way! Being an entrepreneur requires the same resolute commitment as summiting Everest. Just imagine me as your productivity Sherpa.

The goal of this step in the **Revolutionary Productivity Process** is to capitalize on, and follow through to completion, all of the hard word you've put in up to this point.

It's time to take a look at your business operations moving forward, create a plan, and commit to it. Commit to using the new systems you've created. Commit to using the new technology you're delegating to. This step is all about *commitment.*

Commit to Your Success

Believe it or not, there are small business owners who will work hard to set themselves free, eliminate chaos, overhaul their *TnT*, document their systems, and delegate to technology and team—and then do *nothing* with it.

It's heartbreaking.

I know that you are going to see this through to the summit, so let's talk straight, one mission-passionate entrepreneur to another.

Here's the deal. Humans are creatures of habit, and it's so easy to backslide into old habits, even when you've spent the time and energy to create new ones. That's why I'm taking a stand for you and your mission.

Raise your right-hand and repeat after me.

(Seriously!)

> *I solemnly swear that when I backslide I will keep going. I acknowledge that everyone backslides and makes mistakes. Even though I'm a total rock star entrepreneur, I am not immune to this. When I backslide, I promise to immediately forgive myself, laugh it off, return to my commitment to have a revolutionary small business, and keep going. Mastery comes from repetition. I will repeat what I've learned until I master it.*

I know it's easy enough for me to say, "Create new habits! Don't backslide!" but it's something else to actually equip you to go the distance. So, I'm going to give you some tools and strategies to help you follow through on your commitment.

In his book, *Miracle Morning*, Hal Elrod shares three phases to the 30-day process of creating a new habit.

1. *Unbearable Phase:* This is the first ten days, where starting a new habit is a painful struggle. This is where a lot of people give up.

2. *Uncomfortable Phase:* This is the second ten days of the process. Things are no longer unbearable, but they are not yet comfortable either. You're about to break through, so keep going!

3. *Unstoppable Phase:* In the final ten days you cement your commitment to your new routine. Once you reach this point, you will begin to reap the rewards of your efforts in earnest, so it's easy to commit to continuing your new habit well beyond the 30-day mark.

I love this three-phase process because it allows you to have realistic expectations about starting a new habit. It reminds you that there is light at the end of the tunnel, and that the longer you stick with your new habit, the easier it will become.

Another important strategy for starting a new habit and keeping it going is using *triggers* to remind you to take the new action you want to adopt.

A *trigger* is a pattern interrupter. Let's say you're establishing a routine for creating your e-mail newsletter at the same time every week. A trigger for this could be creating a calendar event for this task, and setting either a calendar event alert or an alarm on your phone. Other triggers might include visual cues likes notes, a printed checklist on your desk, or making a change that disrupts your old pattern and makes you consciously think about your newsletter.

As my dear friend and mentor Fabienne Fredrickson always says, "You don't get results from things you don't implement fully."

Now that you've committed to following your new systems and habits, what happens if the process—or, heaven forbid, the technology—changes?

Have no fear. I'll address this in the seventh and final step of **The Revolutionary Productivity Process**: *Adapt for Success*.

Chapter 10
Adapt for Success
(REVOLUTIONARY PRODUCTIVITY PROCESS™ STEP SEVEN)

There is a pervasive misconception in our culture that, once something is organized or systematized, it should forever stay the same. This is a recipe for failure.

Nothing in life, including systems and productivity, are static. Your business is a constantly evolving entity.

Maintenance

If you bought new boots that didn't fit on your closet shelves, would you blame and abandon your closet? No. That would be silly. You would find a solution that created more space for your new boots.

When change happens (which it inevitably will), you must be *proactive*, not reactive. Someone who responds reactively might blame the system for failing. Someone who is proactive will acknowledge that a shift has occurred, and make whatever adjustments to current systems are necessary to keep themselves in the **Revolutionary Zone.**

Always expect that systems are going to change and transform. Create a plan for change, and a protocol for how frequently and in what ways you will update your systems. This is very important to the long-term success of your company, because it will ensure that your systems and processes are continuously evolving with you.

Gather all of your documented systems and processes into one Microsoft Word® document that will serve as your company's Operations Manual. Having all of your systems in one place makes them easy to update. Then, ensure that you and your team members read through your Operations Manual once a quarter to identify any areas that need to be updated. (You should also update your operations manual before hiring a new team member.)

Your goal as a small business owner should be to help your team feel autonomous and invested in maintaining your company's systems.

For example, if one team member sends out your e-mail newsletter every week, that person should know how to update your Operations Manual so that, when the e-mail marketing platform technology changes, they can immediately update the e-mail newsletter system in the Operations Manual.

This continual adaptation of the system also prevents panic when a team member leaves the company without updating the systems they managed, or telling you what they changed.

Strategic Growth

A primary key to continual growth is to periodically evaluate, broaden, and deepen your delegation to team and technology.

When deciding how and when to delegate, remember to keep your alignment as you learned in the *Eliminate Chaos* step of the **Revolutionary Productivity Process**. Once you have the entire **Revolutionary Productivity Process** in place, delegation is the best tool for realigning your priorities, goals, and schedules if your alignment shifts.

Over time, you will see more income coming in. You will see more lives changing.

Eventually though, no matter how diligent you are at implementing the **Revolutionary Productivity Process**, you will eventually hit a ceiling in your growth. When that happens, it will be time to start the process anew at Step One: *Set Yourself Free.*

Embracing your commitment to continually grow, adapt, and revisit your boundaries and priorities is like receiving the keys to the entrepreneur kingdom.

Before you spread your beautiful wings though, I have some words of caution for you …

Chapter 11
Pitfalls: A Word of Caution

Being a mission-passionate entrepreneur is a full-contact sport. It can shake you down into your soul, but it's worth every minute.

Earlier in this book, I shared with you some statistics about small business failure rates. It's pretty scary stuff—but you don't have to be a statistic.

My hope and prayer for you is that you are the "anomaly"—the victorious warrior, the one in two businesses that survive those first five years. I hope you do more than survive. I hope you *thrive*.

I understand it's not easy. Even armed with the **Revolutionary Productivity Process**, you may still feel intimidated by the future. I get it. But this is a safe place to explore your fears, concerns, and potential pitfalls, and prepare for them.

Common Mistakes

If there's one thing I know about being an entrepreneur, it's this: what you don't know that you don't know is often what takes you down.

I've seen many entrepreneur friends and colleagues burn themselves out and even close their businesses because they were committed to "figuring it out" on their own. They weren't willing to invest in themselves, their businesses, and their missions to learn what they didn't know they didn't know.

We each have a unique set of gifts and talents that bring something distinct and necessary to the world. If organizing, systematizing, and delegating are not your unique strengths, then you need support to accomplish them. It's that simple.

Do you remember our analogy of building a city? All of those waterlines, gas pipes, parks, and trash removal systems need to be present in your shiny new city if you want to create an environment conducive to success and world transformation. The same is true of your business. If you don't make sure your foundation is stable, there's no guarantee your company will last. You could quickly find yourself in an inescapable sinkhole.

Something else entrepreneurs do frequently is play the blame game. They blame themselves for being "failures" when really, it's all about the wiring they were born with. Self-blame also lets them sit and lick their wounds instead of doing something about their business's problems.

Another huge and avoidable mistake is investing in a team before you know exactly how you're going to delegate to them and what systems you have in place. If you do that, you will waste time and money, and you might even waste a valuable team member if you end up parting ways because you didn't have your act together. Hiring before you have your systems in place is not worth it.

In the same vein, blaming your team for lack of growth, disorganization, or lack of systems is not appropriate. It also does not accurately label or fix the problem. If you didn't hire your team specifically to create systems for you, don't expect them to do it with excellence, if at all.

After all of this, you may feel discouraged, like you're stuck in the bottom of a pit. You may be thinking, "How the heck do I get out of this?"

Don't worry. I'm at the top of the pit with a rope ladder. You don't have to stay in that hole if you don't want to.

I've got you.

Chapter 12
Next Steps

It drives me crazy that so many productivity "experts" want you to cram as much into your day and life as you possibly can, with no regard for your family, mission, or need for renewing rest.

I'm calling bull-crap on that!

We live in an era where the paradigm of the world is shifting to love. We each have an important role to play, and that role is *not* being a productivity machine.

You deserve to have a high quality of life. You deserve to transform the many lives you want to touch, and be abundantly rewarded for your service. I know that your mission in the world can be sustainable. You don't have to be stuck swirling in **The Cycle of Burnout**.

What would it mean if you only did what you loved each day? What if you never again had to do all of the dreaded tasks in your company that drain you? What if you and your mission were fully supported by custom systems, processes, team, and technology?

Imagine the ripple effect you could have. You'd transform more lives, which would transform more lives, which would transform more lives. On and on and on, rippling outward on the surface of time. You are the source of love and light.

I know that you want a life that supports your business, and a business that supports your life. That's the true definition of freedom right? An absence of restraint.

I know you can design your life and business on your terms. Like a tapestry, your life is woven into your business; your dreams, goals, and aspirations are woven into your mission; and your mission is woven into the world.

Everything is one.

What Comes Next

I only had enough room in this book to give you the beginning layers of each of the seven-steps in the **Revolutionary Productivity Process**.

Luckily, there is an opportunity for deeper learning if you desire it.

With entrepreneurs just like you in mind, I created the **Revolutionary Productivity Academy™**, where I work with mission-passionate entrepreneurs to help them save *two hours per day or more* in their small businesses.

In the Academy, I'll take a deep dive with you into each step in the **Revolutionary Productivity Process**, and provide guidance, tools, templates, resources, and best practices that show you exactly how the process works. In other words, I'll give you all of the juicy stuff I didn't have room for in this book.

The Revolutionary Productivity Academy is an on-line, 6-month-long interactive learning program. You'll participate alongside a loving community of mission-passionate entrepreneurs who, just like you, are committed to changing the world, increasing their income, and getting their lives back. You will have access to me through Group Coaching calls, a private Facebook group, and monthly Group Coaching/Implementation Days.

Entrepreneurs Are Saying ...

❝ Thanks to Katie and the **Revolutionary Productivity Process,** my team is way more productive, way more efficient ... and I'm way more relaxed in my work life ... It's actually trickling over into beautiful things happening in my personal life, which was a completely unexpected bonus in our work together.

- Lori Fischer, Rethink Home Interiors

❝ The **Revolutionary Productivity Process** is indeed revolutionary. I have been using this powerful process for over a year and a half. There is not a part of my life that it does not touch on a daily basis. When I began using it, I thought, that this would be just another productivity model to follow that would make me more, well, productive. I was so mistaken!

Yes, I am much more productive having streamlined much of what I do into actionable systems. But, I do so much more in alignment with my hopes and dreams than ever before.

Katie Mazzocco has given, from her heart, a true gift in sharing the **Revolutionary Productivity Process**. With its use, you are infusing your own dream and desires and love into action. Ultimately, you become more *you*! I'm forever grateful for having worked with Katie using this exact process she is sharing. With her grace, she clearly understood what my needs were, we laughed through the use of these steps creating amazing results for me.

Do the action steps she shows here and watch your world transform as you save two hours a day or more in your business.

- Laura Clark, Soul Wise Living

This is the power of Revolutionary Productivity. It is not about doing more-more-more, but about how to set up systems to bring more ease, abundance, and joy into your business … which can't help but spill over into other areas of your life.

(By the way, when implemented, Revolutionary Productivity will allow you to *start* having a personal life!)

Ultimately, it's about raising the consciousness of the world. When you're in stress and chaos, it suppresses your ability to be creative, and to listen to your intuition. It's time to be present, savor and enjoy your life, and bring your world-changing mission to a larger stage.

I am *not* a productivity expert. I am a systems strategist. Productivity for the sake of activity means nothing without a strategy that delivers you the freedom that sent you down the entrepreneurial path in the first place.

I am so thrilled to be on this journey with you! Please let me know how I can be of service.

Visit www.RevolutionaryProductivityAcademy.com to discover how the Revolutionary Productivity Academy™ will transform your life and business today!

Resources

Join the growing number of revolutionary entrepreneurs using Katie's seven-step **Revolutionary Productivity Process**, which guarantees that you will save *two hours per day or more* in your small business!

Revolutionary Productivity Academy™
www.RevolutionaryProductivityAcademy.com

Mission-passionate entrepreneurs join the **Revolutionary Productivity Academy** not only to save *two or more hours per day* in their businesses, but also to discover exactly how to make more money, transform the world in a bigger way, and get their lives back.

Using the **Revolutionary Productivity Process,** you can stop burning out and have the life and business you dream of. Through this six-month online academy, you too can revolutionize your productivity in a loving, supportive community of passionate entrepreneurs.

Visit the link above to learn more!

On Social Media

Facebook: www.Facebook.com/FSProductivity

Twitter: www.Twitter.com/FSProductivity

YouTube: www.YouTube.com/FSProductivity

LinkedIn: www.linkedin.com/in/klmazzocco

Katie is active on Facebook, Twitter, YouTube and LinkedIn. She loves to engage in meaningful conversations, inspire and support entrepreneurs in leading the lives they dream of. Visit the links above to connect today.

Book Katie to Speak!

Book Katie as your next keynote speaker and you're certain to revolutionize your productivity while discovering how to maximize your time, impact, and income in your small business.

Katie Mazzocco has been leading, laughing with and inspiring audiences for more than four years, and has helped thousands with her energetic and results-oriented messages. She believes that entrepreneurs are here to transform the world and it's her mission and passion to help small business owners, like you, transform more lives by being more productive.

As the creator of the **Revolutionary Productivity Process** and founder of the **Revolutionary Productivity Academy,** Katie is resolute in her belief that people, especially entrepreneurs, are not meant to be productivity-machines.

Your productivity and "success" should not be measured and scrutinized by cold inputs and outputs, rather your productivity should be defined by what Katie defines as **The Revolutionary Zone.** From this place your business, personal life and mission find balance and sustainability, which prevents you from falling victim to **The Cycle of Burnout**.

Her expertise has been sought out by the award-winning learning platform, Curious.com, where she is their resident small business productivity expert.

For more information, visit
www.FullSpectrumProductivity.com/speaking

About Katie

Katie Mazzocco, the Small Business Systems Strategist, is the founder of the **Revolutionary Productivity Academy™** and the creator of the **Revolutionary Productivity Process™**.

In her Revolutionary Productivity Academy, Katie teaches her proven, step-by-step system that teaches small business owners how to increase their income and impact in the world by saving two hours or more per day in their small business. She believes that entrepreneurs are here to transform the world by growing their mission an leading with love in all parts of their lives. Katie is on a mission to start a revolution by teaching entrepreneurs how to keep from burning out, while showing them that life, even as a small business owner, can be balanced, enjoyable and abundant.

www.ingramcontent.com/pod-product-compliance
Lightning Source LLC
Chambersburg PA
CBHW060639210326
41520CB00010B/1666